# E. BLAGRAVE
# TILT

## POEMS

*Cormorant Books*

**Canada Council** **Conseil des Arts**
**for the Arts** **du Canada**

ONTARIO ARTS COUNCIL
CONSEIL DES ARTS DE L'ONTARIO

The publisher gratefully acknowledges the support of the Canada Council for the Arts and the Ontario Arts Council for its publishing program. We acknowledge the financial support of the Government of Canada through the Canada Book Fund (CBF) for our publishing activities, and the Government of Ontario through the Ontario Media Development Corporation, an agency of the Ontario Ministry of Culture, and the Ontario Book Publishing Tax Credit Program.

LIBRARY AND ARCHIVES CANADA CATALOGUING IN PUBLICATION

Blagrave, E.
    Tilt / E. Blagrave.

Poems.
ISBN 978-1-77086-099-5

I. Title.

PS8603.L2959T55 2012     C811 .6     C2012-900280-1

Cover art and design: Angel Guerra/Archetype
Interior text design: Tannice Goddard, Soul Oasis Networking
Printer: Sunville

Printed and bound in Canada.

Cormorant Books Inc.
390 Steelcase Road East, Markham, Ontario, L3R 1G2
www.cormorantbooks.com

*To the memory of my father,*
*Doug Blagrave*

# Contents

# TILT

POEMS

## Tilt

Tilt, the tumbling doves,
  white and grey
  among the green trees.

Tilt, a blind man's head,
  the whispering silk
  of his lady's dress.

Tilt, the hanged man's neck,
  the gingery root
  the sting of hemp.

Tilt, the knife edge of
  the axis, poling
  to Antarctica.

Tilt, the random tiles
  out of the cup
Tilt, your face for
  a kiss.

## The Gifts

Bring me river tigers
    with dreams to eat
    and magic

bring me open cages
with glittering birds
black ravens' eyes
and duck down

bring me foam flecked
    streams
    and aspen leaves

More than the world;

bring me river tigers.

## For Rob

The laburnum brushes the horse's ears
with yellow clusters
and conjures up
the tints of your love.

Your eyes,
lapis lazuli
fixed and followed
the brown horse and me.

In your absence,
the horse, unbridled
carries me
but I have wished
to pass some other tree.

On aimless horses
such as this
and under trees
that seem no more
to shake themselves
because of us,
our love is left to time
to braid the yellow clusters up;
to give to me what isn't mine.

## Summer Latitudes

Horses swarm like the tide
    on the grassy hill
    sparking, flying
around you, asleep
under the apple trees.

## Orchards

Orchards; the careful arrangement, the inheritance of an ancestor's geometrical eye.

When we swing on knobbly branches the ground flies up at us and we land, a three-point landing, and smiling in our resting place we take a sight down the acreage and find a straight line of apple trees like a column of soldiers. We take comfort in such precision. It gives us an inkling of our situation.

A hundred and fifty years ago a fragile great-grandfather set down spindly seedlings in a row. He must have seen us at this moment under thick old trees playing in the avenues, being part of his toil and his own straight lines.

So we inherit decision and power. Through love and time we take aim and unthinkingly rush between the trees to become, victoriously, part of the pattern.

## Gatineau

A dove flew down
    like a cannonball bird
Mid-afternoon into
    Queen Anne's Lace.

Mid-afternoon
    among broken grass
    and golden stubble,
Haymakers humming
    to a hot blue sky,
I watch while a dove
    plays crazy,
    divebombing
    white flowers
    with a lunatic eye.

## Chestnut and Grey

My horse has eyes like garnets,
    fiery under the moon.

Pony, trumpet for your love when
    the moon is full.

She's just a dark mare down in the
    dry shade breathing the
    scent of tumbleweed.

My horse has feet like thunder agates
    and he roars when the sun
    hits the plain.

Pony, call to your grey mare — she
    comes with a hide like glass.

Call to her when the moon is full
    and her eyes are as green
    as grass.

My horse, he's a thousand shades of red
    when the midwinter sun
    breaks the cloud.

Pony, here's your grey mare; she
    comes like a ghost,
    in foal.

Call to her when the moon is full
    and her eyes are beaten brass.

## The Sea Gull

There was once a sea gull of green.

A bright night gull
fetching and coming in with the
logs shaken upon the tide.
He was like a light in the
harbours of houses.

The once timely branch made him a wing
buried in the air.
The once buried sword made him a beak
stirring the sun.
The grasses made him green.

The sea gull moaned about these islands
like a parted wave,
grasping trees by their tops
with his yellow yellow feet.
We could seek his dismal shape
in the winds of kites.

He landed only in the marshes
near the windmill.
He greedily followed the sails.
The children would hunt
the marshes
to crack his emerald neck in two
or climb the windmill to break
the yellow claws,
while the sea gull wailed over their hands.

The gull beat out to sea to come in
on the logs at night.
He was green like the sea weed.
His legs were yellow canes.

He is like the tide.
He gallops under the moon.
His groans are murderous.
His fishing loses ships.

## Night Walk

The full moon is fogged
    (a sign of tomorrow's
    poor weather)

The salty hedges
    crammed with smells
    guide us down
    to the river.

Night is pale
    and flat
like the moonfaced
cows
who browse
at the edge
of the river

You and I
    are shadowed
    like old cinemascope,
    hot and moving;
    brown as
    the river.

## He led me

He led me under a grey fir tree
surrounded by thorn
branch and bough
He had the moon and sky for me.

How to catch fish when the air grows cool

with branch and thorn
with bed and bough
the fish will wander
into your pool
glimmering eyes
steely fin
then you pull the
white fish in
with branch and thorn
with bed and bough
a criss-cross line
ravel and spin
oh love of mine
pull the fishes in
with branch and thorn
with bed and bough.

## Song

If I could come to you sometime
all on a cold dark night
up through the junipers
and follow the stream
crouch like a frog
green green like a leaf of watercress
I would glow in the in between of the trees
and be blind
and be dumb
and feel not     but the trill of my tongue
and the earth bearing me round.

## Past Tense

His dream comes out at night;
a wanderer down a grey road
mistaken for somebody;
and suddenly the sharp smell
of the marsh.

She frightened four birds
in the rushes with her clear laugh.
The boat spun.
What finery — the bullrushes flashing.
The turtle brooded in the spin
and kept his silence.

## Riddle

He's a puzzle
    heard through veils
    like water through stone —
    clouds of rain;
    in the dry places,
    rock and bone.

In the flat lands
    see him come
    only a finger-length
    high
    yet riverwide —
    see the grass lie down.

## Sooke River

The rains fell,
    the river swelled and Clara,
    she dove and took wing.

The stream-bed is red, the bird
    has a white breast — Clara's
    hair is a tangle of watercress.

Up the wet, blue rock into the pool,
    Clara went glad. In her white
    skin with the round breasts
    into deep water went Clara.

The river rose and washed away
    the tangle of watercress,
    and Clara

Mad as green moss swam after
    down the high falls.

## He was fairer than corn growing

He was fairer than corn growing
and brighter by far than the dawn
he took her in hand like a dove
and he led her down
led her down
to the sea-shore.

I watched from the cold blue tower
I waited beside the stone
while he took her in hand like a dove
and he led her down
led her down
to the sea-shore.

I was queen of my own habitation
It was upon my own land
I saw my love kissing
another woman's hand
woman's hand
by the sea-shore.

The clouds they have rain in plenty
and the moon can shake the tide
the wind was a raven of fury
as they stood side by side
side by side
on the sea-shore.

They had hell in all of their kisses
they were doomed under my own hand
for they drowned by the three kind servants
who came at my command
my command
to the sea-shore.

## Cut my dreams loose

Cut my dreams loose.
Sever the worst.

Hand them off
    to the brave
    who challenge
    the hard wind
    that blows hereabouts.

I've had bad and good
    but I swear
    my awakening
    is harsh.

The nights pass
    without lamp
    or light
but what's worse
    is the day
when dreams
    evolve
from blind reckoning
    into white.

## Madam Black

madam black
on the right
clear footing

the way is seen
to be sucked in
the darkness;
the cage; the bird with a mane;
the din of bats
gain you one half-league
in a full league of men.

through the wooden bars,
madam black
see your way clear
under the claws
of the striped one.

oh madam black
your sweat and the tear
coming off the sinew
of your face,
you carry Striped One on your back.

madam black, madam black
red-eyed mare
with your nostrils
discovering the cage
and your mane blown with bats;
a league of men one half-league behind
and Striped One heavy on your back.

### Thin and narrow ...


Thin and narrow as a cage of pale bamboo
wet as the ferns that grow there
she inhabits the hollows of the wood
and she stares.

I have seen her covered in rotten earth
and heard her coming sideways
through the willows when the sun's gone
and fled from the sound.

Every night my dreams open to her pale eyes.
She looks into them with her hands
curved over the sill
and bends her huge head
down and in.

The nights will drag by
till the undergrowth
is consumed
and I, in her stead,
keep the hollow home.

## Ghosts

They tremble in the air
   like smoked glass.
Some strike the stones
Some ring with cold
Some beat the air
   blue and yellow gold.

I had a ghost
   who danced
   a tic-toc gait
and pulled the moon
   a ball of straw
   down glimmering
   upon the snow.

## The Soul Catcher

The blue souls hang in the trees,
knocking branches; a dry thin sound.
Her dark skirts catching juniper bushes
the red seeds roll behind,
the soul catcher follows the scent like a hound.
Into firs, into night she's gone.

Flat and silent, the blue souls grow breathless and dim
revolving each one in its turn.
The soul catcher follows the scent
like a knife      blind, swift she goes
she runs moonless
red berries fall from her gown.
At the grove she pauses
and listens      with one arm
tears the blue souls down.

## I have penny-weights

I have penny-weights,
everyone,
I weigh stones that
men walk on.
I deal out the price of
coals
To warm such lame men's
bony souls.

this lame man had a treasure of stars
he forfeited all for one black coal
all he holds is a cinder of time

i keep those stars in a heap of fire
and measure them out on my penny-weight scale
i have reckoned their worth in terms of years
my diminished stars will be coals for hire

I have penny-weights,
everyone,
I weigh stones that
men walk on.
I deal out the price of
coals
To warm such lame men's
bony souls.

## Tell me my speech

Tell me my speech
   doesn't make me poor;
   less than a singing bird.

I sense a weakening
   in our rapport

and the moon knows
our pale climbing
is not effortless

Our mouths are stunned,
   dumb
   with no rhyme
   or reason.

### The soft blind moths

The soft blind moths
trembling and love-sick
search for their
ladies and desire.
The moon is tugging
the things that climb,
the cornered angels
beat their wings
while we design
hour after hour
on the oppressing walls
our lovers
and the world outside.

## You are so alone

You are so alone in the next room.
The strings, the gentle creatures feed on air.
I stood by the cold window
and saw how the dark comes here.

The shapes of faces were everywhere
among the chimneys.
The sky was white with snow.
I saw one of its eyes through a chink
in a great wood wall.

On the south sides of buildings
the murk gathers in.

You sing one song.
I remember all this before.
It was going to be like this always.

The buildings are chained
and have in them lonely places.
The faces among the chimneys gather
with the snow, cloud and follow each
and one another here below.

## The Floor

The floor is not level
   here.
It slopes a bit;
    tables wobble
    and a marble rolls
    eastward.
Mind you,
    I teeter
    from time to time
    and slide like
    slate
    or skate on
    smooth surfaces.
Drawn to high places;
    it only takes a leg
    over the edge
    for me.
This floor is not level.

## Bipolarities

### i   See-Saw

The morbidity of
diminishing returns.
Dwarf and Giant
planted in flesh
complete and born
under the sun
where all things
normal
are busy with
all things normal.
But the shadows
cast by these
see-saw twins
straight from the womb
sun-spotted
clean to the bone
make us all, normally,
crooked as a thumb.

## ii  Like Kites

We sail
like kites

in our dreams

landscaped
in streams of light;

a wavering gel
shimmering
in a cell-for-cell
trade-off
of lunar black
for lunar white.

### iii  Supine

Chase, chase them away
    the ones who tell
    who catch you at it

I live in a waterland
    mutable
There's no place here
    for punctuation
    or truth
    only sleep
    and the cry of birds

Perpendicular I am not
No explanation

Keep them away

### iv  Rattle

Stars break the sky,
   shiver into parts
   unseen by the
   human eye.

When a child,
   I could hold
   one word, one day.

Now words and days
   rattle in my hand
   and split into thousands.

## A Buoyancy Test

Not mad
    but swimming like men
    half drowned

A buoyancy test
    still breathing?
    losing ground?

Wallowing as I do
    I've lost points,
    feel a touch of weed
    and like a plumb
    sink down.

## Before I Was

I knew I was a sot
   before I was,
   to liquid I was born.
My lake was iron fed
   golden water
   fish streaming.
I lay on the floor in the deep
prisms abounding from my eyes.

## Thief

The tangled moon
    smears the ground
    with pale design.
The trees rear up
    like lions
    clawed and maned.
Night birds sounding,
    owling and beading.
They are dark, unseen
 like chivvying ghosts —
I stand by an open window
    and see the light
    that stole my dreams.

## Double

This double face
ghosting in the night-time mirror
is not my daytime face.
More stone.
More eyes.
More bone.
I hope when we
come face to face
and I am old,
I hope she hails me
as a friend
and I'm not left
with an empty glass —
More death, alone,
and full of sorrow
for my dark image past.

## House Dream

Who lives in this house
    jagged with endless
    stairways
    and cardboard boxes

Whose papers curl in
    the corners

Why so grey
    windowless
    crooked floors
    floors that puff
    up dust

Is this a monument
    a testimony
    of a life?
    mine,
    all mine.

## A Wish

Now and then, in womanhood
I wish to be again
   as straight and beloved
   as the cornflower
   as light as milkweed silk
   and to watch
   year for year
the loons on the lake
when the new mists arise.

## Dad

He hated conflict
   having been through war.
Hard and soft
he drew himself in
like the turtle
legs and head
But his heart
was easily cracked
like an egg.
Profound love
   beat against the tides
   seemed to make the moon grow
He understood me
   knew what made me
   rampage through the night.

## A Late Ear

Fall among the corn rows,
    the tassels like
    fine hair
    pricking the air.
The green leaves
    sharp as blades;
    bitter smell,
    yellow beads.
Hidden there
    a maid's prayer:
One husk for a man
    two for a child
    three for the Virgin,
    Mary mild.

## I have hung all the birds

I have hung all the birds
in the fir trees.
These stiff unyielding
flightless things
shine like chunks of
paradise.
Procne with her brass wings
trapped on a screw of wire
has made the world
come to life and sing.

## In the Spaces

Poking through
poking under
all that soil.

Shiny things
in the spaces
digging;
sprigs of horns
smoking hot
cold to touch
wet roots colliding,

insectile clicking
grinding the planet,

blindly shoving
and smoothing
all that soil

Heaving
antediluvian
and moving.

## Sporadic

Cold winds
    and bursts of sun so warm
    you felt like spreading your coat
    to catch the heat,
rather like starlings on the wires,
    who stretch their necks and wings
    to catch, like crocodiles,
    the dawn.

## Reveille

The light charged the day with colour
and the green grass
softly lay
   and the blue sky
   flew above
   with birds and dandelions
   and foxglove tall
   and sweet pea
   every imaginable hue
and the cry went forth
for every man to rise
and do.

## Idle / Idyll

Deep in the sweet barley
    I lie,
the nodding shoots
    springing back.
Foreshortened, my
    toe sits up
like a disassembled
    piece of a
    larger puzzle.
The sky is wet blue —
    clouds of torn silk.
The smell of honey
    thick in my nose.

## All Day the Rain

Soaked and greened
  the garden.
Pattered and spattered
  the window.
The leaves were like tiny
tympanic membranes
bouncing and throbbing.

The day felt like a small room,
compact and jittery.
It quivered with the rain.

## In Deep

Deep in the woods
    hunted by trees
    laced up by branches
    sewn up with undergrowth,

I stumble, catch my hand
    on something
    sharp;
    deep cuts in the web.

There are potholes
    in the forest
    I fall into,
    grasping jagged pine
    to stay upright;
    holes that mark
    where a tree has died.

This is the thick forest
    of my dreams.

## Before the Bell

Afraid of that and this,
of murder, of death,
and twists in my life,
this is as far as I go.
Death comes closer.
Sever the ribs,
deliver me in pieces.
The experts know how to go.
I fear the end,
the slow recess.

## A Second

It started last year;
   growing pains,
   and a gathering.
I may never get it;
For a second
   I thought —
but the minutes
pulled me in,
The tired old song,
   so I found
   myself as alone
   as anyone could be.

Sparrows setting sail
starlings all among;
the ocean, that silky back
that slides in and out;
and all of us alone.

## Here lie

Here lie the agencies
    of my heart:
The still lake
    and the small fish
    simmering therein,
    the sun in my fist,
the drowned world
and all that spins.

**I Have Loved You**

The masted rigging
    of a tree
    is aloft
    with birds.
In its branches the sun
    at noon is
a single shifting light
    dancing on knife points.

I have loved you these seven years.
Time drips like water on a stone.

## I catalogue the books

I catalogue the books
I make my bed of leaves
I live in a century
    of turmoil;
    but I'm told
that in the hills
there's a grove of trees
and in that grove
there's a stone
and on that stone
the faint signs
of sacrifice.

## Am I

Am I the yellowing leaf
   or the water meadow
   drowning me as
   yellow leaf.
Am I the silt that rises
   or the lake that discloses me.
Am I the tree
   or the binding root
Do I leap to the hook
   or hide in the murk
Am I the well or the cup
Do I run or stand still
   when the earth shakes me.
Do I take my heart
   or does my heart take me.
Am I brick or mud.

## We shift

We shift shapes
   willow-backed
   fox-wise
   mute as the hare.

None of us stays fast.
   Now and then
   still as breathless reeds,
   but mostly rocking,
   swallowed in darkness,
   feeling and knowing,
   testing muscle
   and soft bone.

We are curved in position,
   ready to become.

## Presence
### (for Lyn)

I grew in my garden petunias
bright as a bird;
a hollyhock,
and the soft grey beginnings
of pimpernel.
A gentle skinny-legged flat-backed deer
appeared in my garden. Now
I have no hollyhock, no petunias,
and no pimpernel.
Oh but the dear deer
is a lovely critter,
and I am both honoured and saddened
by her presence in my garden.

## I Should Be Asleep, But

there is this
shit-kicking October wind
attacking the building and roaring
around corners — thrilling —
too exciting to sleep —
I don't want to miss a
minute of it.
It is hurling dry maple leaves
at the side of the house
with a dry-bones rattling sound;
spooks are afoot,
firecrackers popping and snapping —
pre-Hallowe'en and sirens hooting —
altogether festive.
I'm no fan of parades
but I love this rush
and slap of wind.

## November

The little tree
was butter-yellow,
was fall.
Fall still graced my window.
After a while the leaves
turned black at the edges
like a blighted rose,
and frost was on the roofs
in the morning.
Then the leaves fell
and winter closed the door.

## Twilight

Wandering through
   and amongst
   the willows,
   water and soft ground.
Down hill and home.
It was a long walk
   through thorns
   and sticky boughs
   the curdling clouds
   the threat of rain.
The cattle are called home
   the fox to her den
   the badger
   tooth and claw
   to his sett.
There is a tug at the heart.
In the end
   who will call us home.

## Trust

I'm not built that way
of water and stone
of air and cloud
but built of earth
and the soft
furrows and
loam.
I treated myself
well, from time to time,
but oftenest
indifferently
and sweeping away
the false hope
that plagues me
I deliver these
few poems
into your hands.

## Acknowledgements

Eight of these poems appeared previously in *Undercurrents: New Voices in Canadian Poetry* (Cormorant, 2011).

"For Rob," "Chestnut and Grey," "The Sea Gull," "He led me," "Song," "Past Tense," "Sooke River," "He was fairer than corn growing," "Madam Black," "Thin and narrow," "The Soul Catcher," "I have penny-weights," and "You are so alone" appeared in *The Fiddlehead* in 1973. "A Wish," "I have hung all the birds," and "The soft blind moths" appeared in *Versus* in 1976.

In more recent years, "Bipolarities," "Tilt," "Am I," "House Dream," and "I have loved you" appeared in *The New Quarterly*; "Ghosts," "Tell me my speech," "Here lie," and "The Gifts" in *The Fiddlehead*; "Gatineau" and "I catalogue the books" in *ARC* (the latter also featured as an *ARC* postcard); "Night Walk" and "We shift" in *Contemporary Verse 2*; and "Summer Latitudes" in *The Antigonish Review*. My thanks to the editors of these publications.

Thank you to Fred Louder, who was there at the beginning.

I feel a strong sense of gratitude to Robyn Sarah, who made this book happen.

## About E. Blagrave

Elizabeth Logan Blagrave was born in Edmonton in 1950. An air force brat, she moved frequently as a child until her father retired to Victoria where she finished high school. At nineteen she moved to Montreal and lived *la vie bohème* for a few fondly remembered years, assisting in theatrical productions and writing poems that appeared in magazines during the 1970s. After some travel in Europe she returned to Victoria, working for the government and later as a sound and lighting technician at the McPherson Playhouse. She began writing again around 2003. *Tilt*, her first collection, brings together new and old poems.